Contents

Some words are shown in bold, **like this**. You can find out what they mean by looking in the glossary.

What is an island?

An island is a piece of land surrounded by water. There are thousands of islands around the world. Most of them are found in oceans, but there are also many in rivers and lakes. Islands range in size from tiny dots of rock or **coral**, to enormous Greenland, the biggest island in the world.

Some islands, such as the Ile du Bac in France, are found in rivers.

Island Life

Anita Ganeri

Raintree is an imprint of Capstone Global Library Limited, a company incorporated in England and Wales having its registered office at 7 Pilgrim Street, London, EC4V 6LB – Registered company number: 6695582

To contact Raintree:
Phone: 0845 6044371,
Fax: + 44 (0) 1865 312263
Email: myorders@raintreepublishers.co.uk.

Text © Capstone Global Library Limited 2013
First published in hardback in 2013
First published in paperback in 2014
The moral rights of the proprietor have been asserted.

Edited by Nancy Dickmann and John-Paul Wilkins
Designed by Richard Parker
Original illustrations © Capstone Global Library Ltd 2013
Illustrations by HL Studios
Picture research by Mica Brancic
Originated by Capstone Global Library Ltd
Printed and bound in China by CTPS

ISBN 978 1 406 24944 6 (hardback)
16 15 14 13 12
10 9 8 7 6 5 4 3 2 1

ISBN 978 1 406 24945 3 (paperback)
17 16 15 14 13
10 9 8 7 6 5 4 3 2 1

British Library Cataloguing in Publication Data
Ganeri, Anita.
Island life.
306'.09142-dc23
A full catalogue record for this book is available from the British Library.

Acknowledgements
We would like to thank the following for permission to reproduce photographs: Alamy pp. 7 (© Tom Mackie), 11 (© Frank Siedlok), 22 (© Chris Pearsall), 28 (© Hilary Morgan), 29 (© Guy Harrop), 31 (© Iain Sarjeant), 35 (© George Munday); Corbis pp. 4 (Hemis/© Francis Cormon), 27 (Frans Lanting); Manx Heritage Foundation p. 17; Photoshot pp. 8 (Pacific Stock), 12 (Ashley Cooper), 13 (LuisLiwanag/WpN), 14 (David Robertson), 18 (Ian Murray); Shutterstock pp. 9 (© Urosr), 16 (© Tupungato), 19 (© Ho Philip), 21 (© John de la Bastide), 32 (© Ryan M. Bolton), 38 (© Maria Skaldina), 40 (© Karin Claus), 41 (© Haider); SuperStock pp. 5 (© Universal Images Group), 20 (© Robert Harding Picture Library), 23 (© Photononstop), 25 (age fotostock/© Michael S. Nolan), 30 (© imagebroker.net), 36 (age fotostock/© Julian Brooks), 37 (age fotostock/© Ragnar Th. Sigurdsson).

Foreground cover photograph of a girl reproduced with permission of HillCreek Pictures (Erik Buis). Background cover photograph of Canna School on the Isle of Canna, Scotland, reproduced with permission of Alamy (© Tom Kidd). Cover photograph of a summer landscape with sea and blue sky reproduced with permission of Shutterstock (silver-john).

Every effort has been made to contact copyright holders of material reproduced in this book. Any omissions will be rectified in subsequent printings if notice is given to the publisher.

Disclaimer

British Isles

The British Isles are a group of islands that lie off the north-west coast of mainland Europe in the Atlantic Ocean. The biggest island in the group is Great Britain, which is divided into the countries of England, Scotland, and Wales. The second largest island is Ireland.

More than 6,000 islands make up the British Isles.

Island story

Some islands are too small and wild for anyone to live on. Others are countries in their own right, with large **populations**. On some islands, people still follow traditional lifestyles, living off fishing and farming. Life can be difficult, especially if the islands are **isolated** – islanders may have to leave their homes to find work on the **mainland**.

Island types

There are two main types of islands – continental islands and oceanic islands. Continental islands lie along the edge of a **continent** and are part of that continent. The other type of islands, oceanic islands, are found far out at sea.

Continental islands

Continental islands form when the sea floods a section of the coast, cutting off a piece of high land. This high land becomes an island, separated from the **mainland** by a stretch of water. Many of the world's biggest islands, including Madagascar, Sumatra, and Great Britain, are continental islands.

Great Britain is part of the continent of Europe. During the last **Ice Age**, a huge sheet of ice covered a lot of Europe. About 10,000 years ago, the ice melted and caused sea levels to rise. This water eventually formed the English Channel, which separates Great Britain from the mainland.

Did You Know?

Some islands, such as St Michael's Mount in Cornwall, England, are only islands at high **tide**. When the tide goes out, it is linked to the mainland by exposed rocks and sand.

St Michael's Mount only becomes an island at high tide.

Islands in the ocean

Oceanic islands are found far out at sea. These islands are not part of a continent. Most of them are the tops of underwater **volcanoes** that grow up from the seabed. These volcanoes are built when **magma** leaks up through cracks in the seabed. The volcanoes gradually grow taller until they break through the surface of the water.

Island story

In November 1963, a cloud of smoke, ash, and **lava** began rising from the sea off the south coast of Iceland. Local fishermen watched in amazement as a brand-new island was born. It was named Surtsey, after a Norse fire giant, and was formed by a volcano erupting underwater.

The island of Hawaii is made up of five volcanoes, including Kilauea (above).

Coral islands

The Pacific Ocean is dotted with thousands of tiny **coral** islands, called **atolls**. An atoll begins when a **coral reef** grows around a **volcanic** island. Over millions of years, the volcano wears away and sinks, leaving the coral behind. Atolls are often horseshoe-shaped, with a deep, blue **lagoon** inside.

Rangiroa is a coral atoll found in the South Pacific Ocean.

Island environments

The islands of the British Isles have some amazing scenery. Anglesey is a large island off the north-west coast of Wales. It is separated from the **mainland** by a stretch of water called the Menai Strait. The island is famous for its beautiful sandy beaches, dramatic cliffs, and small bays.

As the wind and waves crash against the coast, they carve out dramatic features, such as cliffs, caves, arches, and sea stacks. The Needles is a row of three white chalk stacks that rise out of the sea off the Isle of Wight, which lies off the south coast of England. They get their name from a fourth, needle-shaped stack which collapsed in a storm in 1764.

Island story

The highest sea cliffs in the world can be found at Kalaupapa on the island of Molokai in Hawaii. They plunge more than 1 kilometre down into the Pacific Ocean.

Fingal's Cave is a sea cave on the island of Staffa, Scotland. It is made from six-sided blocks of basalt, a type of **volcanic** rock. The cave has a large, arched entrance.

Weather and climate

The sea has a huge effect on the weather and **climate** of islands. Ocean **currents** carry warm or cold water around the world. One current, called the Gulf Stream, carries warm water from the **equator** to the North Atlantic Ocean. This has a warming effect on the climate of the British Isles.

Tropical plants can grow on Tresco, one of the Isles of Scilly, due to the warming effect of the Gulf Stream.

These people in the Philippines are leaving their homes because of flooding caused by a typhoon.

Serious storms

The Philippines is a group of more than 7,000 islands in the Pacific Ocean in South East Asia. The islands lie right in the path of fierce tropical storms, called typhoons. Each year, between May and November, the storms batter the islands, causing flooding and mudslides. Because the islands are far out in the ocean, they are not protected from the destructive winds and rain.

ISLAND FOCUS:
Isle of Barra

Barra is a small island in the Outer Hebrides, a group of islands off the north-west coast of Scotland. Ferries bring visitors and supplies from the **mainland**, and run from island to island. There are also flights to and from Barra airport. Planes use the beach as a runway, so they can only land and take off at low tide.

Barra's airport provides an important link to the mainland.

Island people

About 1,300 people live on Barra. Many people still speak the ancient language of Gaelic. Traditionally, the islanders worked as herring fishermen or as farmers, called crofters.

Today, some islanders leave the island for long stretches to work on the mainland. Others earn their living from tourism. Each summer, thousands of vistors come to the island to enjoy the beautiful sandy beaches, stunning scenery, and amazing wildlife.

Barra fact file

Location: Atlantic Ocean
Land area: 90 square kilometres
Main village: Castlebay
Island group: Outer Hebrides
Population: about 1,300

Island fact:
The highest hill on Barra is Heaval, at 383 metres tall. About half-way up stands a white marble statue of Mary and Jesus, called 'Our Lady of the Sea'.

Life on an island

Life on an island depends on whether the island is large or small, **isolated** or easy to reach. On small islands, communities are often very tightly knit. People know each other well – they look out for each other and join together to celebrate special events.

The town of Moskenes is found in the Lefoten **archipelego** in Norway. A **ferry** harbour helps keep it connected to the mainland.

School days

For many island children, going to school is just like going to school anywhere else. Smaller islands, however, may only have one school for the whole community. Some children may have a long walk to school or have to go to the **mainland** to continue their education.

There is no secondary school on the Chatham Islands in the Pacific Ocean. Some students stay at home and study by **distance-learning**. But most leave the island and go to boarding schools in New Zealand.

Did You Know?

The Isle of Man is a small island off the west coast of England. It has its own language, called Manx, that is not spoken anywhere else. The islanders all speak English but children also learn Manx at school. At one school on the island, children do all of their lessons in Manx.

Bunscoill Ghaelgag primary school in St John's is the only school on the Isle of Man that teaches all of its lessons in Manx.

Jobs and work

On many islands, people make their living from the seas around them. They catch fish to eat and to sell. The Shetland Islands lie off the north-east coast of Scotland. Fishing is very important for the islands' **economy**. On other islands, people farm oysters and other shellfish.

Each year, Shetland fishermen catch more than 75,000 tonnes of fish, such as mackerel.

Island holidays

Islands all around the world are popular places to go on holiday. Millions of tourists flock to islands such as the West Indies to enjoy the sunny **climate** and sandy beaches. People also like to visit small islands for peace and quiet. The **economies** of many islands depend mainly on tourism, and many islanders work in the tourist industry.

Island story

Singapore is a tiny country in South East Asia. It is made up of Singapore Island and 60 smaller **islets**. Despite its size, Singapore is a world centre of **finance** and industry, and has one of the busiest ports (pictured here) in the world. Around 140,000 ships arrive each year, carrying millions of tonnes of goods and passengers.

Celebrations and traditions

Island celebrations are often linked to events in the island's history. Each winter, a spectacular fire festival takes place in the Shetland Islands. It is called Up Helly Aa and is a reminder of the islands' Viking past. Hundreds of islanders go on a night-time torchlit **procession**, dressed up as Vikings and dragging a model of a Viking longship through the streets.

Did You Know?

Every two years, thousands of islanders gather for the Island Games. First held in 1985, competitors come from 25 islands all over the world, including St Helena and Rhodes. They take part in sports such as athletics, sailing, and cycling.

At the end of the Up Helly Aa procession, the torches are thrown into the ship, setting it on fire.

Carnival!

In February or March, the Caribbean islands of Trinidad and Tobago explode into colour as Carnival comes to town. Groups of islanders dance and parade through the streets to the catchy sound of **calypso** music. They dress in dazzling costumes and are led by a king and queen, whose costumes are even bigger and grander.

At the Carnival in Trinidad and Tobago, there are competitions for the best music and costumes.

Transport and supplies

Because islands are surrounded by sea, transport between islands is usually by boat. **Ferries** are regular boat services, bringing passengers, post, and goods from the **mainland** and other islands. For **remote** islands, these ferry services are a lifeline. If they cannot run because the sea is too rough, the island may run short on vital supplies, including food.

Island story

The Isle of Skye in Scotland is connected to the mainland by a road bridge. The bridge was opened in 1995, and crosses 500 metres of sea. One pillar stands on the tiny island of Eilean Ban, using it as a stepping stone.

This ferry links the Isle of Wight to mainland Great Britain.

No cars

No cars are allowed on Sark, which is one of the smallest of the Channel Islands. Passengers and goods arrive by ferry, then are transported by tractor-drawn buses. The only other vehicles allowed are horse-drawn carriages and bicycles.

Horse-drawn carriages and bicycles are traditional forms of transport on Sark.

Did You Know?

The islands of Honshu and Hokkaido in Japan are linked by the 53-kilometre-long Seikan railway tunnel. Almost half of the tunnel runs under the seabed, making it the longest and deepest rail tunnel in the world.

ISLAND FOCUS:
Tristan da Cunha

Tristan da Cunha is a tiny **volcanic** island in the South Atlantic Ocean. It is one of the most **remote** islands on Earth. Most of the island is mountainous. The highest point is the peak of the **volcano** that forms the island. It is called Queen Mary's Peak and stands 2,062 metres high.

WELCOME TO THE

TRISTAN DA CUNHA

SOUTH ATLANTIC

REMOTEST ISLAND

ACENSION ISLAND
1741 MILES

MONTEVIDEO
2123 MILES

ST HELENA ISLAND
1343 MILES

INACCESSIBLE ISLA-
22 MILES

CAPE TOWN
151' '' ES

LONDON
5337 MILES

OSLO
5915 MILES

FALKLAND ISLAND
2166 MILES

Tristan da Cunha lies more than 2,800 kilometres from the nearest land in South Africa.

Tristan da Cunha fact file

Location: South Atlantic Ocean
Land area: 98 square kilometres
Capital: Edinburgh of the
   Seven Seas
Island group: Tristan da Cunha
Population: 310

Island fact:
In 1961, Queen Mary's Peak **erupted** and all of the islanders were **evacuated** to England. Most of them returned when the island was declared safe two years later.

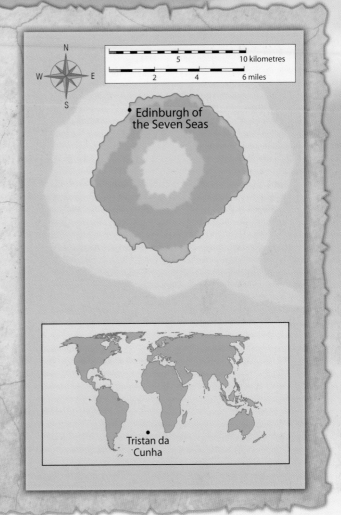

Island life

Only a few hundred people live on Tristan da Cunha. Settlers arrived there from Britain in the early 19th century, and the island is now part of Britain. Because of this, the islanders speak English.

Most people work in local government and in the crayfish industry. The island also earns money by selling postage stamps and coins. There is no airport on the island. Mail and other supplies are brought by boat from South Africa. The island now has a British postcode so that the islanders can order goods on the internet.

Island wildlife

Many islands have been cut off from other land for millions of years. This has meant that some island wildlife cannot be found anywhere else on Earth. Madagascar is a large island in the Indian Ocean. It became separated from **mainland** Africa about 160 million years ago. It is famous for its unique animals, especially its lemurs.

Here be dragons

The world's largest lizard, the Komodo dragon, lives on the islands of Komodo, Rinca, and Flores in Indonesia. It can also be found on some of the tiny surrounding islands in the region. The Komodo dragon can grow to more than 3 metres long. It is an example of an island animal that has grown much larger than it might on the mainland. This is because, on islands, there is less competition for food.

Did You Know?

The Isle of Man is famous for two special animals. One is the Manx Loaghtan, a type of sheep that has dark brown wool and four to six horns. The other is the Manx cat, which has only a short tail or no tail at all.

This ring-tailed lemur, like all other types of lemur, is only found on Madagascar and the Comoro Islands.

27

Island birds

Islands are often used as breeding sites by seabirds. The Farne Islands lie off the coast of north-east England. In the breeding season (from May to July), they are home to around 100,000 nesting birds and their chicks. These include guillemots, kittiwakes, shags, terns, and puffins.

Guillemots make their nests on the Farne Islands' rocky cliffs.

Did You Know?

Some islands are famous for their flightless birds. Many birds fly to escape from predators. Because islands have few predators, birds, such as the kiwi of New Zealand, did not need to fly. Unfortunately, today, they are hunted by animals brought in by humans.

Unwelcome visitors

Islands are safe places to nest because they have fewer **predators**. But if new animals arrive on an island, it can cause problems. Lundy is a tiny island off the south-west coast of England. It was home to thousands of pairs of nesting puffins but, by the year 2000, this had fallen to 10. This was because rats had eaten so many eggs and chicks. It is thought that the rats reached the island from wrecked ships some 200 years ago, and their numbers quickly grew.

A huge operation was launched to kill the rats on Lundy, and the puffins are now making a comeback.

Island plants

Some plants are already growing on an island when it becomes separated from the mainland. New plants also reach islands in different ways. Some seeds are blown by the wind or carried by birds, on their feet and feathers, in their beaks, and in their droppings. Other seeds, such as coconuts, are able to float for hundreds of kilometres before washing up on a beach and sprouting.

Did You Know?

The coco de mer (right) is a palm tree that grows on the Seychelles, a group of islands in the Indian Ocean. It can grow more than 30 metres tall and has the biggest and heaviest seeds of any plant.

These sand dunes on Iona, Scotland, are held together by marram grass.

Plant protectors

Some plants help to protect the coasts of islands from being worn away. Marram grass grows on **sand dunes**. It has long, creeping roots that help to bind the sand together and keep the sand dune stable. Mangroves are trees that grow along the coasts of some tropical islands. They help to protect the coast by forming a barrier against the waves.

ISLAND FOCUS:
The Galapagos Islands

The Galapagos Islands lie around the **equator** in the Pacific Ocean, almost 1,000 kilometres off the west coast of South America. There are 13 main islands and several smaller islands and **islets**. The islands are the tops of underwater **volcanoes**, some of which are still **erupting**. The largest island, Isabela, is formed from six volcanoes merged into one.

Charles Darwin studied marine iguanas when he visited the islands in the 1830s.

Wonderful wildlife

The Galapagos Islands are famous for their amazing animals, many of which live nowhere else. They include giant tortoises, flightless cormorants, and marine iguanas. Marine iguanas are the only lizards that are at home in the sea. They are good swimmers and divers, as they feed on seaweed from underwater rocks. They are able to get rid of any salt they swallow through their noses.

Galapagos fact file

Location: Pacific Ocean
Land area: about 8,000 square kilometres
Biggest city: Puerto Ayora
Biggest island: Isabela
Population: about 25,000

Island fact:
Many unusual plants grow on the Galapagos Islands. Many are thought to have grown from seeds blown to the islands on the wind.

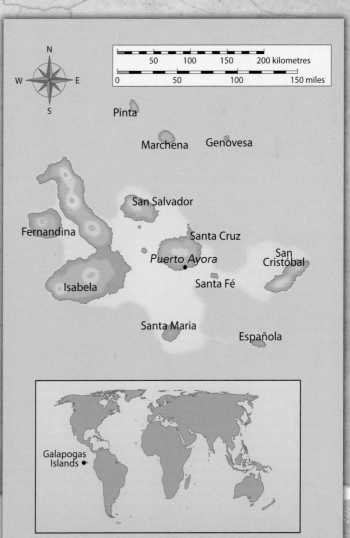

Changing islands

On some **remote** islands, people still live as they have done for centuries. For many islanders, however, life is changing at a fast pace and it has become more difficult to make a living by traditional fishing and farming. Islanders may be forced to leave their islands to find work. If they stay, they must find other ways of earning money, such as running hotels or activities for tourists.

Abandoned islands

The Blasket Islands (pictured right) are a group of islands off the west coast of Ireland. The biggest island, Great Blasket, was once home to 176 people. But the wild weather and harsh conditions made life very difficult for the islanders. Many left to find work somewhere else until only 22 people were left. In 1953, the islands were finally abandoned. Today, tourists can visit the islands and see the ruins of the old village.

Island story

Tourism is an important source of **income**, or earnings, for many islanders but it can cause problems. The island of Zakynthos in Greece is an important nesting site for loggerhead turtles. But tourists are disturbing the sandy beaches, putting the turtles' future in danger.

Great Blasket Island was once home to many famous writers.

Changing landscapes

All over the world, island coastlines are crumbling as the wind and waves **erode** the rocks. In some places, roads and even houses may collapse into the sea. On the Isle of Wight, off the south coast of England, some stretches of coastline are being worn away at a rate of between 1 and 3 metres a year. The problem is being closely studied, and home-owners are being given advice on how to protect their houses.

Parts of the Isle of Wight coastline are crumbling into the sea.

Saving the shore

There are various ways of slowing down the speed of erosion. On the Isle of Wight, some cliffs are protected by planks of wood, held in place by long bolts. Wire netting is also used where the rocks are very crumbly. Another way is to use rock armour. This means piling up large boulders or chunks of concrete at the base of the cliff.

Did You Know?

The island of Iceland (pictured above) is getting bigger. It sits on the Mid-Atlantic Ridge, a line of volcanoes that runs down the middle of the Atlantic Ocean from north to south. Here, two plates of Earth's **crust** are slowly moving apart. **Magma** rises to fill the gap and build new crust.

ISLAND FOCUS:
The Maldives

The Maldives is a small island country in the Indian Ocean. It is made up of more than 1,000 beautiful **coral** islands, which form 26 **atolls**. People only live on about 200 of the islands. Most work in the tourist and tuna fishing industries. Hundreds of thousands of tourists visit each year, and some of the islands have been turned into holiday resorts just for tourists.

The islands' beautiful beaches bring in many tourists, but rising sea levels are a threat.

Islands in danger

Most scientists agree that **global warming** is already making Earth warmer. If it continues, it could melt the ice at the **Poles** and cause sea levels to rise. This would be a disaster for the Maldives. Most of the islands are very low-lying, rising less than 1 metre above the water. Any rise in sea level, and they would be flooded.

Maldives fact file

Location: Indian Ocean
Land area: 298 square
    kilometres
Capital: Malé
Biggest island: Gan
Population: 394,000

Island fact:
In December 2004, the Maldives were hit by a terrible **tsunami** that swept across the Indian Ocean. The enormous waves caused serious flooding and loss of life.

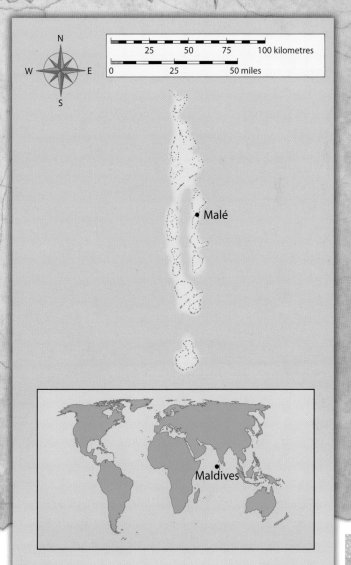

The future for islands

Islands are important for many reasons. Some have amazing wildlife or scenery, and valuable natural resources. Many have a long history. The island of Orkney off the coast of Scotland is famous for the ancient village of Skara Brae. Dating from around 3000 BCE, it was discovered in 1850 when a storm stripped the earth from a hillside and uncovered the ruins of several stone huts.

Skara Brae lies right on the coast. However, before the land **eroded** away, it stood some distance from the sea.

National parks

Today, islands all over the world are under threat, but there is also good news. To protect them, many islands, such as Lundy (see page 29), are being turned into national parks or nature reserves. This means that their unique wildlife and beautiful landscapes will be carefully managed and protected for the future.

Island story

A chain of man-made islands (pictured below) is being built off the coast of the United Arab Emirates in the Persian Gulf. They are in the shape of giant palm trees. They are being made from sand dredged up, or scraped, from the seabed.

The British Isles

N
W   E
S

Lewis and Harris

Orkney Islands

Outer Hebrides

Skye

Inner Hebrides

Barra

Shetland Islands

North Atlantic Ocean

Islay

Mull

North Sea

Farne Islands

Isle of Man

Irish Sea

Ireland

Blasket Islands

Anglesey

Great Britain

Lundy

St Michael's Mount

Scilly Isles

Tresco

English Channel

Isle of Wight

Guernsey   Alderney
            Sark
Jersey   Channel Islands

150   300 kilometres

0   150   300 miles

Island facts and figures

10 largest islands in the world

Island	Area (square kilometres)	Population (approx)
1. Greenland	2,175,600	57,695
2. New Guinea	785,753	6,400,000
3. Borneo	748,168	19,712,000
4. Madagascar	587,715	22,585,000
5. Baffin	503,944	17,000
6. Sumatra	443,066	47,101,000
7. Great Britain	229,957	60,500,000
8. Honshu	225,800	104,000,000
9. Victoria	220,548	2,000
10. Ellesmere	183,965	200

10 largest British islands

Island	Area (square kilometres)	Population (approx)
1. Great Britain	229,957	60,500,000
2. Ireland	70,273	4,722,000
3. Lewis and Harris	2,179	19,918
4. Skye	1,656	9,232
5. Shetland (main island)	969	17,550
6. Mull	875	2,667
7. Anglesey	714	69,000
8. Islay	620	3,457
9. Isle of Man	572	80,056
10. Orkney (main island)	523	15,315

Glossary

archipelago group of islands

atoll circular or horseshoe-shaped coral island that forms around a deep lagoon

calypso lively style of music that is popular on some Caribbean islands

climate usual kind of weather found in a place over a period of time

continent continuous land mass; there are seven continents on Earth

coral hard material made from the skeletons of dead sea creatures, called coral polyps

coral reef large underwater structure made of layers of coral that have built up over many years

crust rocky, outer layer of Earth; the ground you walk on

current huge river of warm or cool water that flows around Earth's oceans

distance-learning doing lessons by post or internet

economy country's finances, trade, resources, imports, exports, and services

equator imaginary line running around the middle of Earth

erode wear away because of the action of the wind, waves, and weather

erupt when lava spurts out of a crack in Earth's crust in a volcano

evacuate move away from a place because it is dangerous to stay

ferry boat that regularly carries goods and passengers between islands or between islands and the mainland

finance country's system of money

global warming gradual rise in Earth's temperature, probably caused by the burning of coal and other fuels

Ice Age period when Earth's temperature dropped and thick sheets of ice covered much of North America, Asia, and Europe

income money received for work or property owned

islet small island

isolated in a very remote place, far away from other land

lagoon area of water cut off from the sea by a coral reef

lava name given to magma when it erupts from a volcano

location place in which something is found

magma hot, molten (liquid) rock that lies underneath Earth's crust

mainland main part of a country or region, as viewed from a nearby island

pole most northern (North Pole) or southern (South Pole) point on Earth

population total number of people living in a country, city, or other area

predator animal that hunts other animals for food

procession group of people moving along in an orderly way

remote far away from large areas of population

sand dune sand that is blown into a tall pile by the wind

tide change in the height of the sea that happens about every 12 hours. Tides are caused by the pull of the Moon and Sun.

tsunami ocean wave caused by an underwater earthquake or volcanic eruption

volcanic something that has formed from a volcano

volcano crack in Earth's crust where lava spurts out

Find out more

Books

How Does a Volcano Become an Island? (How Does It Happen?),
   Linda Tagliaferro (Raintree, 2010)
Living on an Island (Our Local Area), Richard Spilsbury
   (Heinemann Library, 2010)
Living on an Island (Ways into Geography), Louise Spilsbury
   (Franklin Watts, 2012)
The World's Most Amazing Islands (Landform Top Tens),
   Anita Ganeri (Raintree, 2010)
Wild Islands (Horrible Geography), Anita Ganeri
   (Scholastic Children's Books, 2010)

Websites

www.abc.net.au/nature/island/links.htm
A website linked to a TV series about islands around Australia, such
as Lizard Island, looking at wildife, weather, and climate.

www.bbc.co.uk/northernireland/schools/4_11/tykids/islandlife
An interactive website which compares life on two small islands –
Rathlin, off the coast of Ireland, and Hallig Oland, off the coast
of Germany.

www.cia.gov/library/publications/the-world-factbook/index.html
Facts, figures, and other information about islands and countries
around the world.

www.islandgames.net
All you ever needed to know about the Island Games, with lists of
competitors, events, and details of the games held so far.

www.isleofman.com
The website of the Isle of Man, with daily news, weather, events, and information about history and geography.

whc.unesco.org/en/list/1
A United Nations website which looks at World Heritage sites around the world, including the Galapagos Islands.

www.worldatlas.com
A website listing all of the world's islands, with maps and facts and figures about many of them.

Further research

See if you can find some further information on the internet about one of the islands focused on in this book: Barra, Tristan de Cunha, The Galapagos, and the Maldives. How do the people there live? What do they like to eat? What activities or sports do they like to do for fun?

Imagine you have landed on an island far away from home and you have nothing but the clothes you arrived in and some water. What would you do? Think about how you would find food and shelter. Write it down, as well as your thoughts and feelings about the place you have arrived at. Look up explorers on the internet, such as Christopher Columbus, Captain Cook, and Charles Darwin. See how they managed to survive.

Index